GW00863700

Mouse Visor

written by **Anne Giulieri**

photography by Ned Meldrum

It is very easy to make a mouse *visor*.
It doesn't take very long to make
and, when you have made it,
you can wear it right away.
A visor is like a hat
because you can wear it on your head.

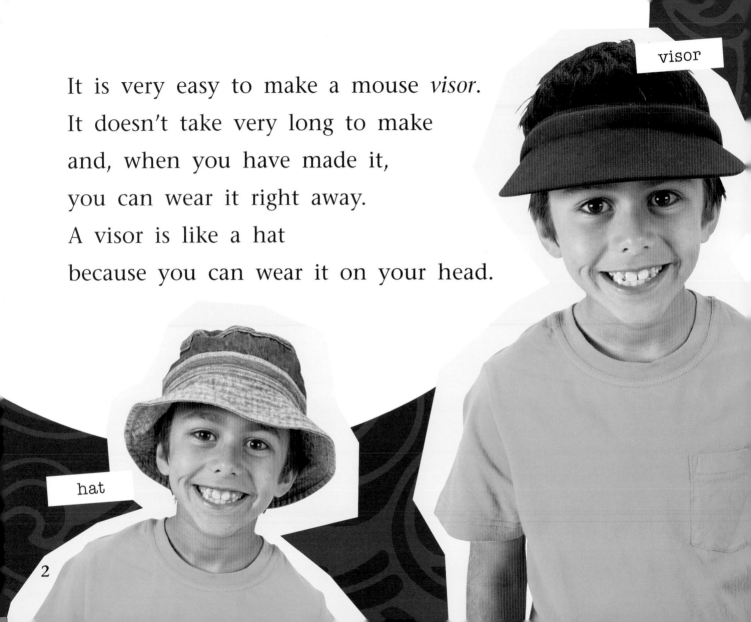

visor

hat

2

To make your mouse visor you will need:

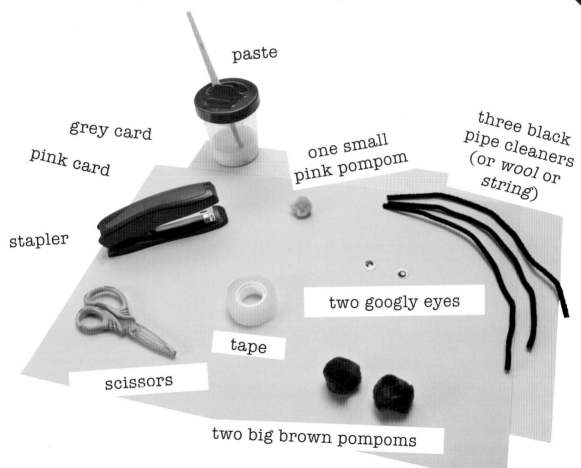

paste

grey card

pink card

one small
pink pompom

three black
pipe cleaners
(or wool or
string)

stapler

two googly eyes

tape

scissors

two big brown pompoms

How To Make a Mouse Visor

The first thing you need to do is to make the *face* and *ears* of your mouse.

Mouse's Face

To make your mouse's face,
cut out a big *shape*
from the grey card just like this.

You will need to make it a big shape,
so that it fits around your head.
This is your mouse's face.
It is also the part that goes around your head.

5

Mouse's Ears

Now cut out two *circles* from the grey card.

These two circles will be your mouse's ears.

Next, cut out two small circles from the pink card.

After you have cut them out,

paste them onto the two grey circles.

They should look like this.

You now have ears for your mouse!

Put Them Together

Now paste the ears
onto the face of your mouse.
You now have the face
and ears of your mouse.

Nose and Cheeks

After you have pasted the ears onto your mouse's face,
it is time to give your mouse a *nose* and some *cheeks*.
Here's what you do.
Paste two big brown pompoms
onto your mouse's face just like this.
These are your mouse's cheeks.

Now paste on the small pink pompom.
Paste it between the two brown pompoms.
This is your mouse's nose.

Eyes and Whiskers

Now paste on the two googly eyes.
These go just down from the ears.

Then carefully cut
three pipe cleaners in half.
This can be hard to do,
so you might need to ask
your teacher for some help.

Now, using some very strong paste,
place the pipe cleaners each side
of the brown pompoms
so that they look like *whiskers*.
If you don't have pipe cleaners,
it doesn't matter because you can use string
or wool instead.

wool

string

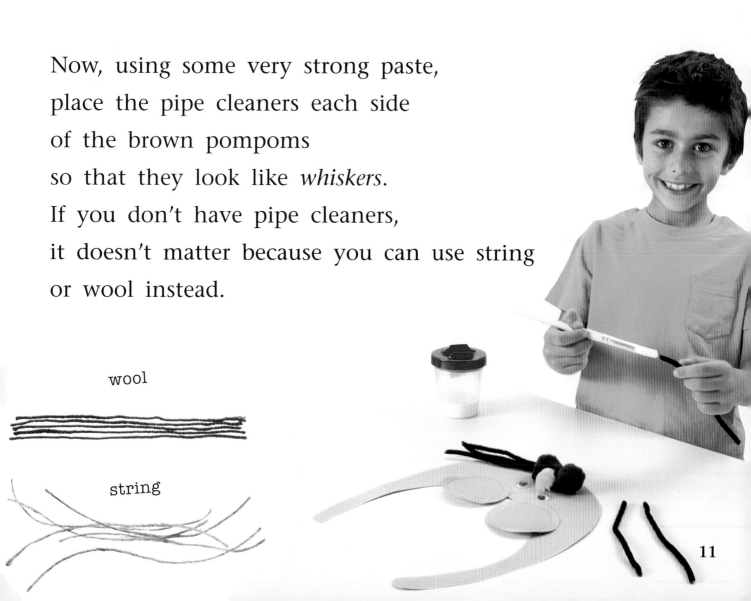

Will Your Mouse Visor Fit?

The last thing you have to do is to see if your mouse visor fits your head.

To do this, put the visor around your head, to work out where the ends need to meet.

Then take the visor
off your head
and ask your teacher
to staple or tape it together.

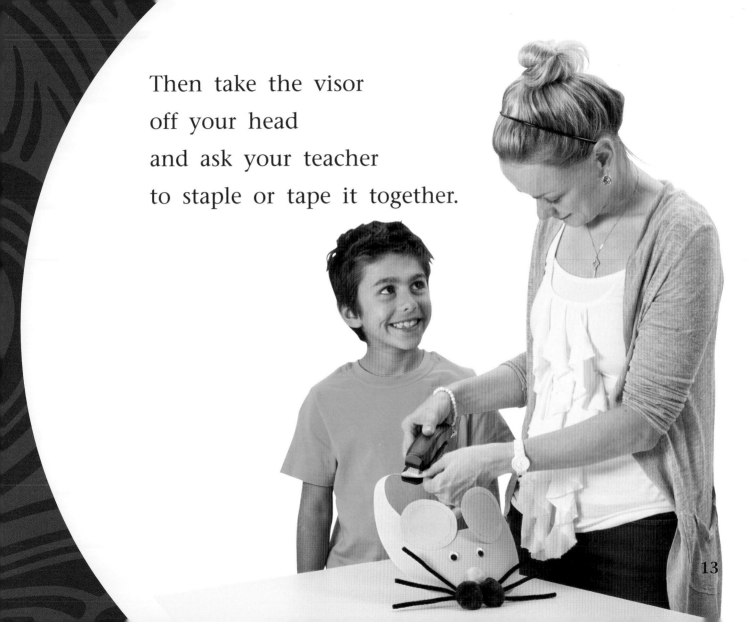

Your mouse visor is now ready to wear.

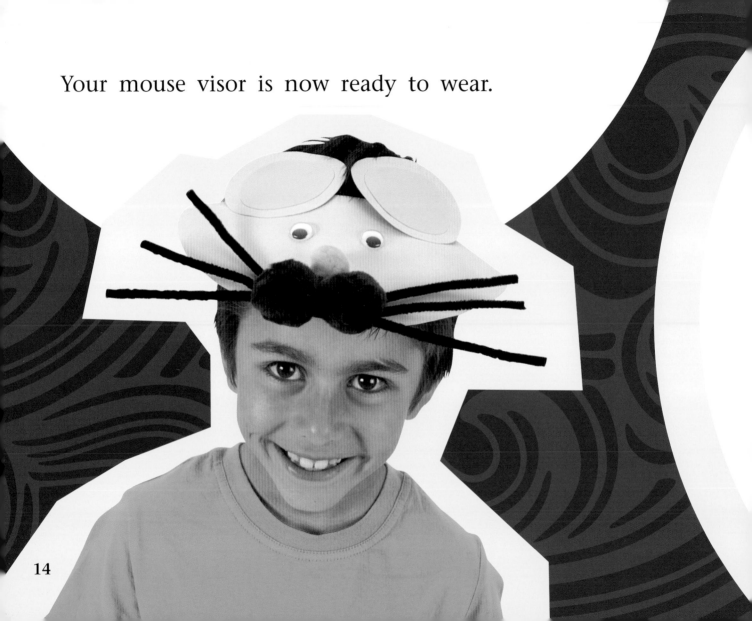

You can make more mice if you like.

Which of these mice is your favourite mouse?

Picture glossary

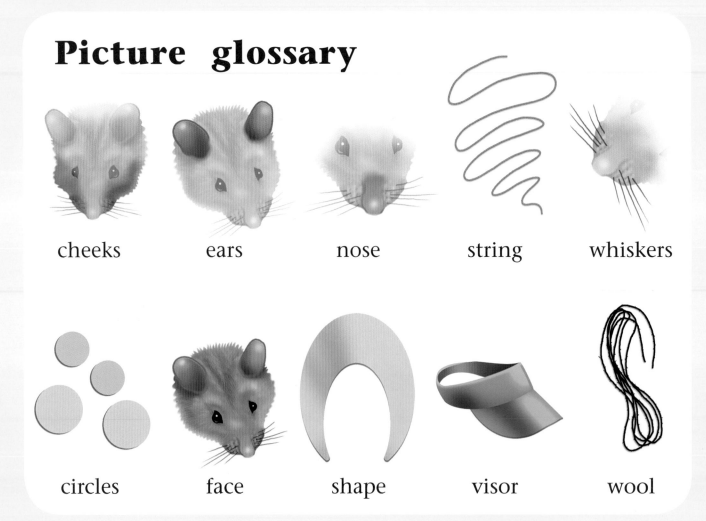

cheeks

ears

nose

string

whiskers

circles

face

shape

visor

wool